CW00357920

SPIRIT OF
NORTHUMBERLAND

JASON FRIEND

First published in Great Britain in 2010

Copyright text and photographs © Jason Friend / Jason Friend Photography Ltd.
Prints are available of all of the images in this book via: www.jasonfriend.co.uk/spiritofnorthumberland

British Library Cataloguing-in-Publication Data
A CIP record for this title is available from the British Library

ISBN 978 1 906887 69 8

PiXZ Books
Halsgrove House, Ryelands Industrial Estate,
Bagley Road, Wellington, Somerset TA21 9PZ
Tel: 01823 653777
Fax: 01823 216796
email: sales@halsgrove.com

An imprint of Halstar Ltd, part of the Halsgrove group of companies
Information on all Halsgrove titles is available at: www.halsgrove.com

Printed and bound in China by Toppan Leefung Printing Ltd

Introduction

Northumberland is not only the northernmost county to be found within England but also the least populated. The 'land of the far horizons' offers some of the most picturesque scenery to be found throughout the British Isles, although it is often overlooked by visitors heading north to the uplands and highlands of Scotland.

Any visitor to the region has an array of locations to visit which all have something to offer. Be it the impressive remains of the World Heritage Site of Hadrian's Wall, the beautiful coastline of the Northumberland Heritage Coast or the rolling yet domineering features of the Northern Pennines as they sprawl towards the Southern Uplands of Scotland, the county can lay claim to a mix of quintessential English scenery.

Although Northumberland is now possibly one of the most tranquil and peaceful spots to be found in England, it has not always been that way. Marauding invaders from Scotland and Scandinavia dictated the construction of numerous fortifications to protect these northernmost English lands. The remnants of these buildings remain dotted across the landscape providing an enigmatic contrast to the natural features of the region.

With the relatively sparse population, and a large amount of suitable habitat, a wide variety of wildlife is found within the boundaries of the county. The Farne Islands are something of a Mecca for the bird watching community, whilst inland areas of woodland host the endangered Red Squirrel that any watchful visitor may have the privilege to see.

The county will reward all of those who visit and allow themselves to experience the Spirit of Northumberland.

A colourful display of pre-dawn colours relected upon the wet sands of Embleton Bay.

Sunset behind the World Heritage Site of Hadrian's Wall
near the town of Once Brewed.

Opposite page:
Flowering heather on the open moorland known as the
Rothbury Terraces, looking towards Simonside.

Northumberland is one of the last remaining
strongholds of the endangered Red Squirrel.

The Clock Tower at Wallington Hall and Gardens near Cambo.

A wire fence running alongside the historic Clennell Steet route,
as it heads towards Alwinton and the Coquetdale Valley.

Opposite page:
Sheep crossing a country road running through dramatic North Pennines scenery.

A row of terraced houses in Warkworth village,
located alongside the Northumberland Heritage Coast.

Autumn colours of woodland within the Cragside estate.

Detail of frost-fringed leaves lying on the floor of a Northumberland forest.

Opposite page:
A winter scene with the remains of snow on the River Breamish,
running through the Cheviots and the Breamish Valley near
the village of Ingram situated within the Northumberland National Park.

View looking from Harbottle Crags Nature Reserve towards Harbottle and Coquetdale.

Opposite page:
Sunset over the rolling Cheviot Hills, viewed from the Border Country Ride route near Murder Cleugh.

A colourful display of autumn colours in the
Allen Banks National Trust area.

Opposite page:
The flowing waters of the Hareshaw Burn
complemented by autumn leaves.

Boats moored within the harbour walls of Beadnell Harbour.

Hexham Bridge over the River Tyne, built in 1793
by Robert Mylne to a design by John Smeaton.

Prehistoric cup and ring marks and rock art located
on a stone at Lordenshaw near the Lordenshaw Hill Fort.

Native ferns below an impressive sandstone ridge formation found on the Kyloe Hills.

The flowing waterfall of
Hareshaw Linn,
a popular spot located within
Northumberland National Park.

Opposite page:
A rocky outcrop found high
above Harthope Valley,
surrounded by a fresh snowfall.

Flowering heather on Birkside Fell near Blanchland, forming part of the North Pennines Area of Outstanding Natural Beauty.

The remains of an
old smelting flue on
Dryburn Moor near Allendale.

A single puffin waits patiently for its mate to return
to their burrow on the Inner Farne Island.

Opposite page:
The Inner Farne Lighthouse was built in 1809 and
is now managed by the National Trust.

Dawn, looking towards the Blyth offshore wind turbines generating a renewable source of energy.

Opposite page:
Incoming tide engulfs the causeway linking St Mary's Island and lighthouse to the mainland.

Female hiker walking towards Carling Crags near the Harthope Valley.

Opposite page:
Lambley footbridge crossing the River South Tyne as it flows through woodland.

The ruins of the impressive Dunstanburgh Castle
situated on a headland near the village of Craster.

Weathered rocks dominate the low-tide shoreline of Embleton Bay.

Sheep grazing in a field in the Breamish Valley near Ingram.

Opposite page:
A winter view of the Great Whin Sill at Cawfields near the town of Haltwhistle.

Thirlwall Castle, near Hadrian's Wall, probably named after the Old English place name of Thirl-Wall which means 'Gap In the Wall'.

The construction of Cragside house, which began in 1863,
was supervised by Sir William Armstrong. Cragside later became
the first house in the world to be lit by hydroelectricity.

The fast flowing waters of the River Allen running through the tree-clad
Staward Gorge estate during the autumn months.

A stream flowing through the autumnal woodland of the Briarwood Banks Nature Reserve.

The remains of Harbottle Castle in Coquetdale.

Opposite page:
Bamburgh Castle and sand dunes near Bamburgh village.

A colourful blanket of flowering native Bluebells and Ramsons (wild garlic).

Hareshaw Burn surrounded by a blanket of leaves.

A fresh layer of snow transforms the woodland of the
Plessey Woods Country Park, located towards the south of the county.

Opposite page:
Warkworth Castle, a magnificent twelfth century stone motte and
bailey fortress, located near the Northumberland Heritage Coast.

The open landscape of the Breamish Valley at the foothills of the Cheviots.

The Cheviot viewed from the route of the St Cuthbert's Way track near the town of Wooler.

Sunset over the mud flats of Budle Bay near Bamburgh.

Opposite page:
Blyth Beach and sand dunes shortly after dawn.

Milestone on the banks of Snear Hill, high above the Harthope Valley.

Typical farmhouse and surrounding Northumberland countryside.

The Forestry Commission-managed woodlands of Thrunton Woods.

Opposite page:
Spring foliage, reflected in the still waters of the River Coquet near Warkworth.

The River South Tyne flowing through a valley of woodland and agricultural land.

Opposite page:
A dramatic stretch of Hadrian's Wall running along the Walltown Craggs.

Lion Bridge near Alnwick Castle which is one of the
finest medieval castles to be found in England.

Cragside house amidst the gardens of the Cragside estate.

Statue of St Aidan in the grounds of the Lindisfarne Priory.

Opposite page:
Lindisfarne Castle situated upon the Holy Island of Lindisfarne.

Bamburgh Castle and dunes
viewed shortly after sunrise,
from a viewpoint on
Harkess Rocks
north of the castle.

Opposite page:
Boats moored in the harbour
at Seahouses, which is known
as 'The Gateway to the
Farne Islands'.

Alnwick Castle, often referred as 'The Windsor of the North',
reflected in the still waters of the River Aln.